C000133022

A gift to

_____

from

_____

Printed edition
Also available in multiple e-book formats

Published by The Endless Bookcase and Changes Forever Publishing House, Suite 14 Stanta Business Centre, 3 Soothouse Spring, St Albans AL3 6PF
www. theendlessbookcase.com

ISBN: 978-1-912243-83-9

Illustrations by Angie Brigden Art
Copy editing by Ilsa Hawtin, WordSure Ltd
Cover photograph by John Woodward photography

A catalogue record for this book is available from the British Library.

The Grief
Garden Path

I dedicate this book to
Richard and Rob

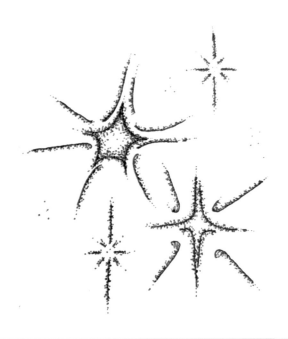

Foreword

By Linda Magistris, CEO/Founder, The Good Grief Trust

Julie has written this insightful and heartfelt book from a powerful place. A place that has a true depth of under-standing, derived from her lived experience and empathy for those who are affected by the death of someone they love. She offers hope, guidance and a unique way of encouraging us to think about our 'garden', our life, that she believes needs tending with care and regular watering. It is a simple, effective analogy, which helps illustrate the importance of self-care when going through a life-changing ordeal, such as a bereavement. We often lose sight of ourselves when we are grieving, so it is vital we find a way to nurture our souls.

Grief impacts your physical, emotional and mental wellbeing. Grief is exhausting and debilitating. It is vital that we ensure our 'garden' can eventually thrive again, and that we are able to move forward through the nettles and enjoy the sunshine when it slowly emerges, albeit through dark clouds at first. With all the stories and little nuggets of advice from others who have been through the trauma of losing someone close, I believe this book will offer acknowledgement, comfort and a way forward for the bereaved, knowing they are not alone in their grief.

This beautiful quote from the book left me with a lovely, warm glow:

> 'Before long, each of their souls took one last flight, soaring high into the clear night sky, where the stars twinkled and shone brightly. Finally, both Peggy and Cybil were free of the bodies that no longer served them.'

Thank you to Julie for your support for our work at The Good Grief Trust.

We wish you all the success in the world x

#StrongerTogether

https://www.thegoodgrieftrust.org

v

vi

Introduction

In my first book, I introduced the analogy of life being like a garden. Just like the plants in a garden, we all NEED to be nourished in order to survive and thrive. It is therefore vial to 'Keep watering YOU' – a phrase I use to remind people of the need to look after themselves, in order to be healthy and happy.

If you ask a child, 'What happens if a flower doesn't get water?', they will immediately be able to tell you that the flower will die. As humans, we are just the same – we have very basic needs, and if they aren't met, we wither and fade. We can't function, and we certainly can't reach our full potential or live our best lives. And eventually, if we don't look after ourselves, we will die.

As humans, our needs are of course more complex – we need to look after both our physical health and mental wellbeing in order to be healthy and happy. All of this is included in my message to 'Keep watering YOU', and it will forever remain the key message I teach to others and practise myself. Whatever the weather in your 'garden' (your life), it will help you to survive and eventually thrive again.

Because you are reading this book, it is likely that you have entered the difficult and challenging process of grief, which I call the 'grief garden path'. Chapter 1 will tell you some more about this process – simply understanding where you are and what you are going through will help you in at least some small way on your road to recovery.

When someone you love dies, you can feel as if you have crash-landed on a different planet. It's not a trip you have planned or paid for, you don't even know how long it will last, and it's certainly not somewhere you would recommend to a friend.

If someone you love dies suddenly, the devastation causes everything and everyone around you to change for ever. Quite simply, nothing remains the same.

Grief happens to everyone who loses someone or something they truly love. It doesn't have to be a person – it could be a way of life, a relationship, a treasured possession, a pet, or something else.

In this book I am particularly looking at the grief at the loss of a loved one. It is my hope that you find something that resonates with you and helps you with what you are experiencing. Maybe it will be a few words, or even a picture, that will give you a greater understanding of your grief garden path, helping you in some way to feel more positive.

The following chapter gives insight into the grieving process. In Chapter 2 you will find a fictional story, which I hope will paint a picture of what you may be feeling or have experienced. After that, I trust that you find some inspiration and reassurance from the real-life stories of people who have suffered different forms of grief, and from their 'golden nuggets of wisdom' – their tips on how to feel better and to look after YOU.

Where are YOU
on your journey along
your grief garden path?

4

Chapter 1

The GOOD grief garden path

The human experience of grief has been studied and written about throughout the ages. In this chapter I will look at two different understandings of the grief process, by Dr Kübler-Ross, from 1969, and by Richard A Dershimer, from 1990. I'll tell you a bit about my own experience of grief, then talk about my analogy, the 'grief garden path', which is a simplified way for you to understand your own grieving process.

While you are reading this chapter, I would like you to consider the following question.

Where are YOU on your journey along the 'good grief garden path'?

Having become a nurse at the age of 17, I was quite young when I first became aware of the stages of grief. During my training, I learned about the work of Dr Elizabeth Kübler-Ross. Her memoirs are incredible, and I remember her talking about her pioneering work in teaching medical students about death and dying. She would even take dying patients into her lectures, for them to share their thoughts and feelings with her students.

Dr Kübler-Ross was able to identify that everyone goes through a grief cycle after losing someone or something they love. This became so well known that it is likely you already have some idea of the different stages identified by Kübler-Ross, as outlined below, each with some examples of the reactions and feelings people experience.

1. **Denial** – avoidance, confusion, elation, shock, fear
2. **Anger** – frustration, irritation, anxiety
3. **Depression** – helplessness, hostility, flight, feeling overwhelmed
4. **Bargaining** – struggling to find meaning, reaching out to others, telling one's story
5. **Acceptance** – exploring options, new plan in place, moving on

Looking now at that list of points outlining the grief cycle, you might already be able to see where you are within the process of grief, according to Kübler-Ross.

My daughters and I started our journey on the grief garden path ten years before this book was published. It all began with a phone call out of the blue, a nursing sister calling to tell me she had some terrible news to share.

The worst thing was the fact that, in that split second, not only had my life changed for ever, but also the lives of my two beautiful daughters. Their father, Richard, had died very suddenly, at the age of 44. He was their dearly loved daddy or, as Amy called it, the other half of her chocolate cake. She described to me when we divorced that if you cut a chocolate cake down the middle, to create two perfect halves, that was how much she loved us both – equally.

Richard's death will probably always remain the worst day of my life. Although he and I had separated prior to his death, I appreciated the impact that his death would have on the lives of our children. Especially hard was that his death was sudden, unpredictable and untimely. Like a tornado, it hit our 'garden' – our lives – leaving nothing the same. There was devastation, everywhere we looked.

I see this as each of my daughters and I at that point experiencing our own pain and beginning our own new path of grief through our garden, our own personal grief process. Each path had been littered with bits of a life once enjoyed, but these were now replaced by challenging and ugly obstacles.

Since that time, I have experienced a very different type of loss – that of my husband, my daughters' beloved step-father, Rob. After a lengthy battle with his health, he died in November 2012. I had become a widow at the age of 45.

Rob's was a more expected death than that of Richard, although I always think we have hope until the very end. Despite everything we know, we continue to hope that the person we love so much will get better, even that they will live on for ever. Rob's death was therefore also devastating, even if in different ways from when we lost Richard.

In 2014 I was invited to attend a workshop for healthcare and teaching professionals, run by Brake, the road-safety charity. As I made my way to the venue, I remember asking myself why I was going, what the purpose of the workshop would be for me.

The first speaker was Crispin, a personal injury lawyer. I was impressed by the fact he used a real-life story about a family he had represented, following the sudden death of a young man on his motorbike. The man had just left home and hadn't even reached the end of his road, when a truck ploughed into him and killed him instantly.

The second speaker was the mother of a daughter who, six months earlier, at the age of 32, had died suddenly. The speaker was still clearly reeling from the shock.

Although those presentations had been incredibly touching, I still hadn't fully appreciated the value of this workshop to me, until the arrival of the following speaker, Dr Stephen Regel OBE. A specialist consultant, he had created a team that specialised in helping those left behind grieving after a sudden death.

Dr Regel explained that sudden death carries additional pain – the trauma of losing a loved one, as well as the trauma of the unexpected event itself. This sudden trauma usually leads to a delay in the grieving process, and everything becomes more complex. For example, in a road traffic accident investigation, the focus and attention can be guided away from the personal process of grief, leaving the relatives and friends trying to overcome the shock of the accident. This often then leaves them at the beginning of the grief garden path rather than able to move through the process and beyond it in a 'good', healthy way. Due to the symptoms of grief manifesting much later, Dr Regel's team often doesn't get referrals until 11 years after a sudden death, when people at last realise that they need help with their grief.

This resonated with me immediately. It was during Dr Regel's presentation that I gained complete understanding of the difference between sudden and unexpected deaths.

Dr Regel also shared his preferred understanding of the grief process, by Richard A Dershimer. Regardless of whether the loss of your loved was sudden or more expected, I hope the process listed below will also help you identify where you are in your journey.

1. Shock
2. Acute grief
3. Straightening up the mess
4. Reinvesting and re-engaging in life

I of course knew about the Kübler-Ross stages of grief, but Dershimer's contemporary model made things very simple and straightforward, allowing me to see where I was at that very moment.

When I attended that workshop, I was still straightening up the almighty mess that had been left behind after Rob's and Richard's deaths. I guess it is why it has taken me another five years to feel ready to finish writing this book.

I want to keep this incredibly simple for you, whatever stage you are at. The process of grief is almost with exception an incredibly challenging and sad journey. However, following the path of grief is necessary, in order for you to go into your future healthy, healed and happy. It then becomes a GOOD grief garden path, rather than an unhealthy one.

On your behalf, I have approached various people who have embarked on and completed their own garden paths of grief. Each of those people is now finally back on earth again in the warm sunshine, safe in the knowledge that their loved one will always be with them in their 'garden' (their life), even if they are now in a different part of the garden. The people telling these stories all feel they will be able to keep their loved ones alive for ever, in their own hearts and minds.

At the end of each story, you will see 'golden nuggets of wisdom' – thoughts and ideas that have helped each person during their own grief process. I sincerely hope that one or more of those ideas will resonate with you and help you on your own good grief garden path.

Before their stories, you will find my own fictional tale, 'The last flight'.

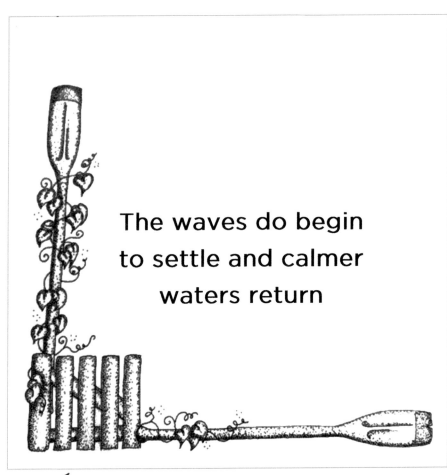

The waves do begin
to settle and calmer
waters return

Chapter 2

The last flight

An old lady called Peggy lived in a Cornish fishing village. It was a tiny place that was crammed full of life.

The inhabitants of the village had lived there since they were born, and their parents and grandparents had lived there before them. As children, all attended the village school, which sat in the heart of their community.

I want you to imagine the beauty of this village, with its church spire reaching for the sky, and the crystal-clear sea, which sparkled when the sun shone.

Fishing was the predominant trade in the village, and the fishermen taking to the seas was a reassuringly familiar sight. Their daily routines took them into known waters, although these could become perilous places when the weather turned. But even in treacherous conditions, the fishermen still took to their boats, travelling far out to sea to catch the fish that sustained their families.

The village was also home to a variety of wildlife. Domesticated cats and dogs lived a life of Riley, being fed and watered by those who took care of them, and enjoying the peace and security of the village and seaside. There were rockpools full of creatures on and around the coastline, and then there were all manner of birds. From black-and-white to brightly coloured feathers, from timid sparrows to friendly robins, from languid herons to dashing peregrine falcons.

The harbour created a haven for the entire village. It was the hub of the community, an enclave of beauty. The fishing boats anchored to their familiar spots, with the chains holding them in place covered with all manner of crustaceans, and with seaweed entwined around the once shiny metal. The sound of the masts clinking in the sea breeze could be heard echoing the age of the harbour – a wonderful, familiar sound – morning, noon and night.

As dusk settled, the clinking of the boats could be heard clearly in the night sky, along with the gentle lapping of the waves as the boats came into shore.

Many seagulls were regular visitors to the seashore, especially in the summer, when there was a rich abundance of food to be gained from the human visitors. The gulls nested in the craggy cliffs along the coastline, from where they would scour the shore and the waves for food, before settling together at night to sleep.

Two of the seagulls became well known to the villagers, who named them Cybil and Cyril. They were beautiful, proud birds, who had lived in and around

the village since they were young chicks, and would wait patiently for scraps of food from the local people.

As seagulls always do, Cybil and Cyril stayed together – a couple enjoying each other's company, looking after each other, and living their lives munching on cockles and other tasty morsels. Over the years, Cybil and Cyril had become proud parents to many beautiful birds, which now also inhabited the shores.

Peggy had lived all her life in the village. Her brother, George, had moved during his life to a different area, but the siblings had remained very close, and George came to visit Peggy from time to time over the years. Peggy had never married, although she had once been engaged to a handsome service man, whose life had ended in the First World War – a hero amongst heroes. She had grieved his loss and yet found joy in the life she lived, in her close-knit community. She was loved dearly by all who knew her.

By the age of 99, Peggy had been living for a few years in a nursing home, together with many other older people from the village. Although George had suffered a stroke, he had made a good recovery and was still able to travel. He now

tended the small window box outside his sister's room in the nursing home.

Peggy's health was gradually deteriorating. One day, the other people in the home could tell that her breathing had changed, becoming more laboured. They also noticed how her chatter and wise words no longer filled the room wherever she was.

Meanwhile, Cybil was also finding it more and more difficult to move, and Cyril fussed about her.

That evening, both Peggy and Cybil took their last breaths. Before long, each of their souls took one last flight, soaring high into the clear night sky, where the stars twinkled and shone brightly. Finally, both

Peggy and Cybil were free of the bodies that no longer served them.

George was by his sister's bedside as she passed away. A tear rolled down his cheek, joining the tears of the other people in the room. There were tears of sadness that Peggy had gone, but also tears of joy for the life that she had lived.

Cyril the seagull was bereft. The partner with whom he had shared nearly his entire life was no longer alive. He flew high into the sky, not knowing where to go, frantically flapping his elderly wings. After a while, his energy ebbed, and he returned mournfully to the seashore. His head sank low into this feathery body.

As the days passed, both George and Cyril deeply felt the loss of those they had loved so much, who had been so significant and special to them for so many years.

The pain they felt came and went, like the waves in the sea. Sometimes the pain felt like gentle waves lapping at the shore, but at other times like six-foot surges, which towered above George and Cyril, knocking them off balance without warning. Those were crashing, thrashing waves, which felt cruel and unforgiving.

The storm of grief is a journey that can seem long and never-ending, but eventually the waves do begin to settle, and calm waters return.

One day on that harbour, the sun began to shine again. It was warm and comforting, and Cybil and

Cyril's offspring could be seen taking flight high above in the sky. The cycle of life, continuing in all its glory.

Being a gardener, George understood the analogy of life being very much like a garden. He knew that Peggy would *always* be in his 'garden', in his life. She had just gone to another part of it, where she would live forever in his heart and mind.

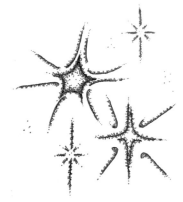

He chose a beautiful pink rose to represent Peggy in his actual garden at home. Each year the rose bloomed more and more beautifully than before. Peggy was gone from life here on earth, but would *never* be forgotten.

Life in the harbour continued, with Cybil and Cyril's offspring soaring higher and higher into the ever-changing skies, while the villagers continued with their daily life on the shore below.

Your loved one
will always be in your
heart and mind

Chapter 3

Real stories of grief

Sarah's story –
the loss of a loved baby

Sarah was married at 26. Soon after, she and her husband decided it was the right time to try for a baby. After six years of trying, and one round of IVF treatment, Sarah and her husband were expecting their first child.

Sarah's pregnancy wasn't considered to be high risk, and all went well until 33 weeks, when, on 18 March, baby Olivia Grace made an appearance.

Olivia Grace was born alive, by emergency caesarean section, but died within minutes. Sarah was at that point unaware of how her life had just changed for ever, as she was still asleep under a general anaesthetic.

Her husband decided he should be the one to tell her the news, and in that moment, Sarah's rose-tinted spectacles disappeared. She says everything went from a world of colour to black-and-white.

Sarah describes feeling shell-shocked and hollow, her arms empty as she left the hospital, leaving the security of the four walls of her room there. Driving home was awful – Sarah could see the spring flowers dancing, but she was returning home to nothing except a nursery with an empty cradle, and with a broken heart.

Sarah says that you think the sun is never, ever going to shine again. She says you want the world to stop turning. You want to scream and shout. She was surprised when friends started to cross the road when they saw her, to avoid awkward conversations.

The years pass by, whether you want that to happen or not. The more time elapsed since Olivia Grace's death, the more distant the memory became, and the more Sarah's guilt set in, especially the guilt she felt if she ever found herself enjoying life again.

Eventually, the flow of life introduced more positive experiences. Olivia's godmother was a tremendous support, visiting or calling every day. Eventually, Sarah realised that she needed some extra help, so she sought professional counselling from SANDS UK, the Stillbirth and Neonatal Death Charity. This was such a huge help to Sarah, helping her own pain to ease, that she even went on to support other parents, as a volunteer with SANDS.

Olivia Grace would have been 22 in the year this book is published. Her mummy and daddy, together with her younger sister, Lucy, who has always known about her big sister, regularly visit Olivia's grave in Wales to celebrate her life.

The flower Sarah has chosen for Olivia Grace is a baby narcissus. Its botanical name is 'new baby'.

Sarah wants everyone to know that the sun is now shining brightly in her 'garden' – her life. She sends you all her love and blessings, at whatever part of the journey you find yourself.

Sarah's golden nuggets of wisdom for you:

- You DON'T get over the loss of a loved one – you learn to live with it and the pain does ease.
- When talking to someone who is grieving, always risk saying the wrong thing rather than nothing at all.
- Men need to cry too.
- Deal with your feelings. Find help in the form of counselling or whatever YOU need. You're not on your own.
- It can be incredibly helpful to create a memory box – a safe place to keep special mementoes.

Julie's story – the loss of a loved child

Julie remembers the day she finally lost that weight of sadness and the sun began to shine again. She had felt guilty about feeling happy. 'After all, how CAN you be happy after losing your child?' she says.

She had spoken to their eldest son, Jonathan, one Sunday night. Julie had been watching *Superman* with her husband, John, when the phone rang. She remembers that last call with Jonathan so vividly.

Life for Julie had been good. After a period of being stressed and unwell, she and John had made changes to their diet, and Julie had adopted a new positive attitude, which was beginning to have an effect.

Julie says, 'What was to come next only happens to other people – it's reported in newspapers or read out by newsreaders. It is difficult to imagine that your own son's death would ever be reported nationally. In fact, the day it happened, the news was reporting the Iraq war and discussing the young men who were going to fight for our country. I remember thinking of the mothers of sons that may never come home.'

It was a day that started like any other and ended like no other. Julie was sitting in the car, waiting for Edward, her youngest son, then aged 17, to come out of his piano lesson. Her mobile rang as she sat waiting, and it was John calling. He asked if she was sitting down, then went on to say that he had just received a call from the Greater Manchester Police, telling him that Jonathan had been involved in a serious road traffic accident. Jonathan had sustained severe head and chest injuries.

'Don't hang about,' John had been told, 'you need to get here urgently.' Julie got Edward and headed for Manchester as quickly as possible. On the journey there, John said, 'It will be okay', trying to reassure Julie. She wasn't so sure; nor was he, really.

When they arrived at the hospital, they were led into a tiny room, greeted with the words, 'There's no easy way to tell you this …', and were told that their beloved son had died 30 minutes before they had arrived. They went to see Jonathan – their beautiful son – where he lay in the hospital chapel, and visited him many times after this.

'The police liaison officer was kind and helpful,' says Julie, 'but what words can help when your child has just died?'

All they knew was that a car, travelling at high speed down the wrong side of the road, had hit their son while he was on a pedestrian crossing. They found out later that, ironically, the last thing Jonathan did was to give a thumbs-up to the bus driver who had stopped to let him cross. The driver of the car hit him and did not stop. The burned-out shell of the car was eventually found, but the driver himself had fled to Pakistan.

John and Julie genuinely didn't feel a sense of hatred, even then. Julie says she even felt guilty for wondering how the driver's life would be affected by his few moments of madness. The driver returned to the UK after several months and was eventually sentenced to four years in a young offenders' institution, for death by dangerous driving. As the judge pointed out at the trial, the driver's sentence was short-term, even though he had killed their son, while Julie and John had been given a life sentence.

Fifteen years later, life goes on and the grief doesn't always show itself; however, it still catches Julie out every now and again. Her faith helps her at these times, and she says that she would always choose to have had 19 years WITH Jonathan rather than not having known him at all.

Julie has chosen a pheasant to represent Jonathan. Soon after his death, a beautiful pheasant appeared and stayed in their garden. It was as though it was Jonathan, communicating a precious message to them that he was still around.

Note: One of the ways Julie honoured her son was through her writing. See *Baring My Soul: A Journey of Faith* by Julie Roberts, ISBN 978-07552-1010-7

Julie's golden nuggets of wisdom for you:

- Your loved one would want you to carry on living, enjoying life.
- Keep talking about them – it keeps them alive.
- Don't let people upset you if they don't know how to respond or what to say.
- Find something to honour your loved one's life, to remember them by.
- There's no point in asking 'Why?' – it prevents you from moving forward.
- Practise mindfulness or meditation and being in the now – it's the way to recognise unhelpful thoughts and learn to let go of them.
- If you are part of a family, you are ALL going through the pain of the loss. Share the pain.
- My mother gave me a little card with the poem 'A Child Loaned', by Edgar A. Guest. I keep it on my dressing table and it reminds me that we don't own our children.

Ian's story –
the loss of a loved sibling

Ian has now retired, after 30 years serving in the police. On reflection, he knows that his choice of career goes back to what happened when he was just twelve years old.

Ian was playing football and, as they always did, his little eight-year-old brother and sister were cycling to come and watch him play. Keith, his brother, was so full of life as he rode carefully up to a junction on the country road he knew so well. But suddenly he was struck by a car, leaving his little body lifeless, like a sack of potatoes, on the road.

Even then, at the age of twelve, Ian felt a strong sense of needing to fight injustice, and he carried this with him right through his working life.

He remembers going home that day, to find Keith's beloved toy soldiers still scattered over the carpet, never to be played with again. Ian and Keith were country boys, who loved playing together outdoors, but now Ian no longer had his playmate. Keith was, quite simply, GONE. Ian describes feeling as though he had lost an arm – a huge void left, which could never be filled.

Ian recalls how, for the rest of his childhood, he had to walk past the car that had killed his brother, parked in the garage of the man who had been driving it. Ian could even see the dent where Keith had been hit.

Ian wasn't allowed to attend his brother's funeral. Everyone was in their own state of shock after Keith's death, and no one talked about what had happened, with each other or with anyone else.

It was only years later, when Ian had retired, that he met Sonya. They shared a passion for cycling, and one day Sonya told Ian how she had felt after her beloved father died. After so many years, Ian felt this was like opening a door, to let little Keith out. Although Keith will be forever young in Ian's mind, through talking about his death, it felt possible almost to bring him back to life and maybe find some peace in the turmoil Ian had compartmentalised for so many years.

Sonya and I met at Harwood Park – a beautiful crematorium, where my husband Rob's koi now happily swim. She was sitting watching them, reflecting on her father, whose memorial plaque is planted with daffodil bulbs, which flower each year. Her father was very clever with words and loved the poem 'The Daffodil'. When I asked if she would be prepared to be interviewed about her loss, she brought Ian along, and he shared his own story.

Ian says that meeting with me, along with the long chats he has had with Sonya, has helped him find some peace in what fundamentally changed him for ever when he was twelve years old. He says that it is only now, at the age of 57, that he is really beginning to fully live life again.

Ian also enjoys the feeling of the adrenalin coursing through his body during his cycling challenges. Maybe he is finally catching up with little soldier Keith on his bicycle and feels able to move forward in his own life, knowing Keith will ALWAYS be with him in his heart and mind.

For Ian, I have chosen Keith's favourite toy soldier to represent him.

Ian's golden nuggets of wisdom for you:

- Talk to someone you trust. Open that Pandora's box. It must come out eventually. (Probably talk to someone sooner than I did! Although, as Julie says, it must be the right time to open the box and begin talking about things.)
- Exercise has helped me both physically and mentally. It could help you!
- Keep something that means something to YOU, relating to your loved one. Keith's toy soldiers meant a lot to me, and keeping them retains a connection with him that will never die.

Amy's story –
the loss of a loved parent

Amy is my eldest child. As mentioned earlier in the book, Amy describes the love she had for her dad and me as being equal, like two halves of a chocolate cake.

When Richard and I separated in 2003, Amy was just ten years old. Separation and divorce are of course forms of loss, and a child has no control over what is happening.

For Amy then to experience the sudden death of her father, in February 2009, was beyond awful. I am grateful that she has wanted to share with you all some of what she has faced and learned about losing a parent.

When she was young, Amy says her life was generally happy and carefree. She enjoyed spending time with her friends and says she didn't have much to complain about.

The day her life changed for ever began like any other school day and ended like no other. She remembers coming home from school, having been picked up by her nanny and auntie. That wasn't unusual, as we are a close family; however, when Amy entered the house that day, something felt different and wrong.

She says, 'I remember my mum kneeling in front of us in the living room and telling us that Dad had died. It didn't really hit me at the time, except I just remember screaming and kind of losing control of my emotions.

'I was in shock and it really didn't feel real until the day after, when we travelled to join my grandparents in the town Dad died. Seeing him in the chapel of rest was some comfort. At least I could touch him and kiss him for the last time. It was a horrific and surreal few days. I understand that not everyone needs to see their loved one, but it helped me.'

Many years have passed since then, and Amy says, 'I still wonder what his last thoughts were, if he had any.

'I have had to continue my life without him. He was very strong-willed, strongminded and funny, and I will always miss being able to pick up the phone and speak to him. He was and is part of me, and I of him, so that will always bind us together.'

Amy says, 'I still get a bit angry when people take their parents for granted. I have had a good support system through my friends and family. Sharing this experience with them has allowed me to feel sad and grieve in my own way.'

She says that she knows it is possible for the sun to shine again. It becomes a bit dark every now and again, but overall the sun is shining.

She is enjoying that sunshine with her partner, Chris. She has resumed her career in primary school teaching, after a restorative two years in Australia.

Amy has chosen a horse chestnut tree to represent her dad. He loved playing 'conkers' as a little boy, and many years ago planted a conker, which has grown into a strong tree on his parents' farm.

Amy's golden nuggets of wisdom for you:

- Time is the biggest healer.
- Everyone deals with their grief differently. For example, my experience was very different from that of my sister.
- Don't take people you love for granted. You don't know how long they will be with you.
- Appreciate what you have and follow your path.

Ilsa's story – the loss of a loved grandparent

Ilsa's mum's mother was affectionately known as 'Granny Bo', or simply 'Bo', at least by her four grandchildren. Bo was unfailingly generous and kind, and had a very strong yet unassuming presence. Everyone in the family looked up to her.

Bo also had a wicked sense of humour. Some of Ilsa's fondest memories are of bursts of uncontrollable giggles amongst the girls of the family, which for some reason only happened when Granny Bo was there, and often at the most inappropriate times.

Towards the end of her life, Bo had multiple health problems. Glaucoma had left her nearly blind, and yet she would do anything to avoid accepting help from anyone. She was in constant pain from arthritis and osteoporosis, but when asked how she was, she would swear she was absolutely fine.

Ilsa says, 'Bo was and still is an inspiration in many ways, thanks to her humour, her stoicism and her rock-solid moral values.'

She continues, 'Due to my dad's work, and later my own, I never lived very close to the village where Bo lived with my Grandad, my aunt and her family. Whenever I went to visit, Bo would be ridiculously grateful, saying what a pain it must have been for me to give up my time. That in itself made the visits even more of a pleasure – I couldn't wait for a free weekend to go and see Bo and to spend time sharing news and life stories.'

Ilsa had just arrived at work one day, when she got a phone call saying that Bo had died. After explaining the situation to her boss, Ilsa jumped in the car to go and join her parents and other relatives. She says she still remembers that journey so clearly, especially trying not to cry as she made her way up the busy M1. Glancing at the commuters in the cars all around her, she wondered if anyone else could be experiencing sadness like hers at that moment.

At the time of writing, it is just over 20 years since Bo died. Ilsa says she is surprised by how much she still misses her, and how small reminders still make her feel incredibly sad. However, she tries to see those moments only as a tribute to Bo's wonderful character, and a reminder of how lucky she is to have known her.

One thing Ilsa has found especially hard is that she met her husband and gave birth to her two children within a few years of Bo passing away. She says she would love nothing more than them all being able to meet each other, to share the pride she feels in both her grandmother and her new family, and knowing that they would all get on like a house on fire. However, she feels that a part of Bo lives on in every one of her descendants, and that they all strive towards her positive take on life. Ilsa says that if she ever feels sorry for herself, she only has to think of an upbeat comment from Bo, and everything feels easier.

Ilsa has chosen the sweet pea to represent Bo. It was her favourite flower, due to its beautiful, lingering scent.

Ilsa's golden nuggets of wisdom for you:

- You don't ever need to 'get over it', to completely overcome the sadness you feel now. Try never to feel bad when grief catches you unawares.
- You'd be surprised by how other people appreciate what you are going through, even if they (or you) don't want to talk about it.
- It really is okay to reach out for help when you lose someone you love. After all, this might be the hardest time you ever face. Whether it's an anonymous call to Samaritans, advice and help from a charity such as The Good Grief Trust, or personal support from a trained recovery coach, there are lots of people who would really love to help you feel better.

Hazel's story – the loss of a loved husband

I am starting this story with a quote from Hazel, which she shared with me when we first started talking. She said, 'Death ends a life, NOT a relationship, and the strong bond remains. It stays with you, even when someone chooses to leave by suicide.'

Hazel and Alan lived together as man and wife for many years, and their greatest achievement together was, and is, their beautiful family – four incredible children.

This story begins one weekend, when the children had gone to stay with their grandparents for the first time. The day felt like any other, but when Hazel stepped out of their bedroom door that morning, she was stepping into a nightmare.

As soon as Hazel came out of their bedroom, she saw Alan's lifeless body hanging from the top of the stairs. He had chosen to end his own life. Everything from that moment was super-charged, heightened, frightening and unknown. Their neighbours were incredible – they called 999, and the police quickly arrived and took over Hazel's altered world, a world that had changed for ever and ever.

'WHY? Why did he decide to leave us now?' Hazel kept asking herself the same questions but couldn't find the answers. There were none and still aren't any. She says that will always remain the hardest thing about Alan's suicide.

She knew she *had* to somehow tell the children – the hardest thing she would ever have to do. When she at last broke it to them that their dad had died, it was her youngest who asked the question, 'Did he kill himself?'

As a parent, how can you possibly answer a question like that? Hazel decided she needed to be as honest and open as she could with her children. She made it her mission to ensure that they always felt supported and listened to, and for them to be given unconditional love every day.

Bruce appeared in their lives and he became a really significant member of the family. Bruce had four legs and wagged his tail a lot! Yes, Bruce was a much-loved dog.

Hazel suppressed her own feelings over the coming years, and says her life has improved immeasurably since she has found ways to talk about everything she has been through. Now she is determined to focus on the path ahead. She says, 'You can look back, but you can't go back. You've *got* to keep moving forward'.

Hazel's biggest fears had always been who would look after the children if anything happened to her. She had to find a job and, over the next 25 years, this developed into a pivotal role within the school in which she worked.

Over the years, her friends and colleagues were always there to listen and to comfort her.

As I write this, Hazel has just welcomed her – and Alan's – eighth grandchild into her life. Hazel's youngest daughter, the little girl who asked that pertinent question all those years ago, has had her second baby, a gorgeous little boy, and brother to his older sister.

The family continues to grow, and Hazel says the sun shines every day. She has started now to think about herself, and she recently chose to retire from the job she loved. She now plays golf again – 28 years after Alan's death, she is learning to live HER life again.

She says, 'He planted the seeds and I did the watering! Life carries on … It's the cycle of life.'

Hazel can now do something she would never, during all the time when she was in such a dark place, have thought possible – she enjoys embracing the seasons in all their glory.

Hazel has chosen a water lily to represent Alan. She chose it because she feels the flower is very serene and beautiful on the surface; however, underneath the roots are a tangled confusion. The water lily is also thought to symbolise love and life.

Hazel's golden nuggets of wisdom for you:

- Take out critical illness cover – get it in place NOW – to safeguard the financial wellbeing of you, your partner and your dependants in case of any unforeseen tragedy.
- After you have lost someone, seek good financial advice, again to safeguard the financial security of you and your family.
- Ask for help, even if you are someone who never normally asks anyone for help!
- Get a 'Bruce' – a four-legged furry friend – he will love you, no matter what!
- Read the poem 'Desiderata' by Max Ehrmann. Hazel was given this on a card and keeps it in her purse. She found some peace in it.
- Eventually, be cheerful and strive to be happy.

Roy's story – the loss of a loved wife

Roy was married to Anita for 32 years. She was not only his wife but his very best friend, always making him feel that he was worth something and belonged somewhere.

They met when Anita's daughter, Anna, was four and a half. The day before they got married, Roy was tucking Anna in for the night, and she said that she couldn't wait for the next day. 'Why?' he asked. Anna replied, 'Because then I can call you "Daddy"'. Their relationship flourished and grew strong, and it wasn't long before Anita and Roy welcomed their son, Richard, to the family.

Anita and Roy's wedding was a hoot, with confetti and dancing the hokey cokey! Roy keeps his wedding ring close to him – it symbolises the love they shared.

The moment their lives changed for ever was with Anita's diagnosis of leukaemia. She fought a brave battle, with Roy by her side every step of the way, but a cure wasn't to be.

The night before Anita passed away, the children went to the shop and bought anything they could find that she liked to eat, including some delicious strawberries. The four of them ate their last meal together that night and chatted a lot; it was such a significant time. The taste of strawberries still reminds Roy of that special night.

Roy was called back to the hospital the following morning. Anita was distressed, and Roy was encouraged to hold her hand. As he did so, he squeezed her hand three times, to say 'I love you'. Anita looked straight at him and smiled. Soon after this, she passed away.

The whole family were deeply affected by the loss of such a strong, central figure. Their son became depressed and was hard to reach; he couldn't talk to anyone. Roy describes feeling completely on his own. No one was talking, everyone in too much pain. Roy explains that they went from being a family to

NOTHING, everyone seeming not to hear or feel each other's pain.

Roy has a strong faith and heard a message that helped him. He believes it was from heaven, and it said this: 'Life is for living – don't waste your life thinking of me. I'm happy where I am, and to be able to see you and our children happy and growing makes me so happy. Kiss my grandson for me. Thank you for all the years we had together. We WILL be together again. Please believe me; I'm not just the thoughts in your head.'

Roy says he loved Anita with all his heart and soul, and that he will live forever with the memories of the good times they had together. He explains, 'What's love? It's that special feeling, so happy to be with that person, content and loved, no matter what.'

As time has passed, Roy has been on a rollercoaster ride of emotions. He had a relationship quite soon afterwards, but realised that he was only ever making comparisons with Anita. He got a dog for company, but soon recognised that wasn't giving him the emotional support he needed. In the end, he just ploughed his way through the emotions that appeared.

Life now is so much better. The love for Anita remains strong; however, the pain of her passing has eased. Roy explains that he has found the peace that he had been looking for in his life, similar to the happiness he had with his wife. It is a sense of contentment in himself.

Their children are also happy, and everyone is back in harmony with each other.

Roy wanted to finish by saying to you, 'Life is never quite the same but you ARE able to move on'.

Roy has chosen an acer tree, or Japanese maple, to represent Anita. He is starting to feel healthy and happy again and, ten years on, has eventually opened the door of his heart to loving someone special.

Roy's golden nuggets of wisdom for you:

- Occasionally, things may happen to remind you of your loved one, for example a film or a piece of music. Allow it to come and go – cry if you need to.
- Let your feelings out – that way you will find peace in your heart.
- You CAN recover and live again, if you allow recovery and healing to happen.
- Look for the contentment in yourself – it *will* come, with time. Then you can move on in your life.

Andrew's story –
the loss of a loved friend

Andrew had finished his university years and was entering the exciting world of work on a regimented international trade floor in central London. His mother believed in tough love and had upped his rent!

One night, he returned home to the comfort of his parents' round table, which is symbolic in Chinese culture of the importance of being able to see everyone during a meal. He even remembers what they had to eat – pork, rice and green peppers.

He remembers his mother being quiet, and then the silence broke with the words from his father, 'Mark is dead'. From that moment, everything slowed and Andrew began to take in every detail. The newsreader on the TV read the headlines about Mark having been kidnapped, tortured and murdered in Rwanda by Hutu rebels. Mark's life adventure had finished before it began.

Andrew had been immediately drawn to Mark when they met, aged 13, at their senior school. They were like chalk and cheese. Mark was an all-As student, quiet and yet funny – so, so funny. Not many people saw that side of him. Andrew says, 'He never judged me for being noisy; he defended me and comforted me.'

Mark's family were Andrew's second family and it was without hesitation, after hearing of Mark's death, that Andrew called and went straight to see Mark's parents, Anne and John; his sister, Emma; and his beloved dog, Chester. Mark had begged his family to get that dog and Chester was very much like his owner – a loyal friend.

Andrew says Chester knew Mark had died. He could see it in his eyes. The Miss Marple house he had spent so much time in while growing up was silent. They were all a mess.

Andrew says that he found it a strange comfort that Mark's death was being reported on the news and headlining every newspaper. It was like the world cared about his best friend.

It was the same at the memorial service at St Albans Cathedral. It was comforting that every seat in that sacred place was filled – so many lives affected by that single ripple, all touched in some way by the man Andrew had looked up to over so many years. He felt it a blessing and an honour to speak at the service, alongside John, who read a poem called 'Just around the corner'. The service was a celebration of Mark's life.

During our interview, Andrew reflected on the fact that, in the six months after Mark died, he ploughed himself into his work. Today, 20 years on, Andrew believes this probably had an incredible impact on his success in business. As he left, he told me he would soon be lecturing at the Harvard Business School. Right now, as I write, I can feel Mark smiling at this.

Andrew explains that he has been on a good grief garden path, as he realises that he hasn't bottled up his emotions. Four years after Mark died, Andrew remembers beginning to cry a flood of tears and quite simply not being able to stop for what seemed like an eternity. He says, 'After that I felt so much better'.

Mark is still remembered and talked about, and Andrew has always maintained strong contact with Mark's parents.

Andrew says, 'Even after such a terrible experience of loss, the sun can shine again. It really can.'

Andrew has chosen Chester the golden lab to represent his loyal friend.

Andrew's golden nuggets of wisdom for you:

- When you are ready to open up, there will be many people ready to hear you and support you.
- Your loved one will always be in your heart and mind.
- Cake – yes, good cake helps!
- Surrounding yourself with the people affected by the loss of your loved one can be very comforting.
- Carry on your 'day to day'.
- Do what feels right to YOU.

Hayley's story – the loss of a loved pet

Hayley has always given homes to 'golden oldies' – older animals that have lost their homes. She has had lots of pets she has loved dearly, though none as special as her beautiful cocker spaniel, Danny.

Danny appeared in her life, aged almost 11, at a rehoming centre. Hayley describes the moment she met him – he had a kind face and he looked a bit lost.

I have always felt that animals feel genuine love for the humans that care for them, as well as pain from grief. The start to this story pretty much confirms what I have always felt.

Danny had been found next to his dead owner, at the home where he had lived since he was a tiny puppy. Hayley says she could see the pain in his eyes. When he was first adopted into Hayley's home, he suffered with terrible separation anxiety and cried like a baby when left alone. Hayley eventually had him sleeping on his bed next to her at night, where he settled quickly and slept like a baby!

Danny is described as a true gent. At first he showed no strong desire to play; presumably, his previous owner hadn't been able to play with him due to ill health. But very soon after arriving at his new home, Danny began to rediscover his love of chasing and retrieving balls. The first picture I saw of him, he had two tennis balls firmly stuffed in his soft, silky mouth. Along with his new lease of life, Danny had of course fallen hook, line and sinker in love with Hayley.

Danny suffered from typical spaniel-ear and dry-eye problems. Hayley took care of his needs as well as cuddling him and walking with him – his feeder, walker and nurse.

After around two years, Danny's health began to deteriorate. It was still a huge shock to all when, quite suddenly, he passed away.

Hayley describes that moment as unbearably painful. Danny had held an emotional and physical space in her home and heart. She missed the noise his collar made when he trotted towards her, and even now she keeps his tag on her keyring.

She says that, even though Danny was only with her for a relatively short time, it felt like losing a partner or a best friend. She felt quite overcome with grief for a long time after losing him. This is an example of why I wanted to include the loss of a pet in this book. Anyone who has had or lost a beloved pet will know that an animal can feel just like a member of the family.

Hayley has now given a home to two other golden oldies, but she knows that Danny will hold a special place in her heart and mind for ever.

When asked what she wanted to represent Danny, she immediately chose a forget-me-not. Hayley never will, and neither will you, EVER forget your loved one.

Hayley's golden nuggets of wisdom for you:

- I was once told something about grief that spoke to me, which I hope will speak to you: 'Life will never be the same; you just have to get used to it being different'.
- Getting another dog didn't stop me from grieving the loss of Danny or make the pain go away any quicker.
- The pain *does* ease.
- You still have a lot of love to give. Don't be afraid to keep sharing and receiving it.
- Listen to your instincts about when it may be right to welcome a new animal into your home. It won't replace your loved one; however, it can bring a sense of peace.
- Grief is the last act of love we can give to those we loved. Where there is deep grief, there was great love.

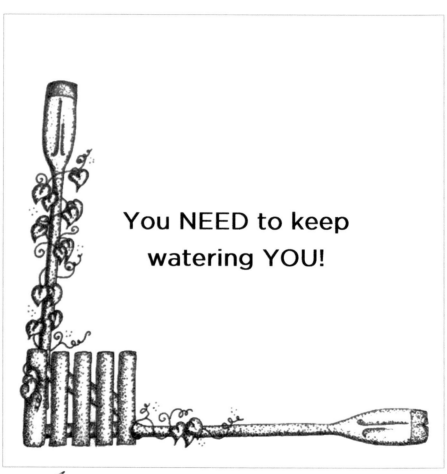

You NEED to keep
watering YOU!

Chapter 4

Keep watering YOU!

I made the decision to use this chapter to explain the importance of my advice, 'Keep watering YOU'. By the end of this final chapter, you will hopefully fully believe the importance of doing this, even when looking after yourself feels impossible, or seems the least important thing to do.

I first realised the importance of 'watering me' in 1998, long before I had experienced significant grief. My children were young, I was working as a nurse and midwife, and I had a home to run and a dog to look after. My list of challenges was considerably longer than that, but I'm sure you get the idea! I eventually completely burned out and couldn't even look after myself, let alone my children.

In my first book, I mentioned how my sister insisted on me joining her on one of her retreats, to give me a necessary break from everything. I would never normally even have considered something like that! But in that amazing week away, I stopped, I sat in the sunshine, I swam, and I read a book. By the end of that week, I was beginning to feel better.

Unfortunately, though, one week away wasn't enough to help me recover. I went straight back into my normal life back at home, and the same happened – I couldn't cope with all the demands and pressures of work, life and looking after my beautiful daughters.

Something clearly had to change.

We have needs, and if we don't address those needs, dire consequences will follow.

I experienced an even harder period, emotionally, later in life. When my husband, Rob, went into hospital for the very last time, I was forced to sleep on the floor of the hospital in order to spend proper time with him. However, I made sure I always got some sleep at home in the afternoon, knowing that I otherwise just wouldn't be able to cope. I would make myself walk my puppy, rather than finding another dog walker, because I appreciated the mental benefit of having time out and fresh air. Despite rushing to get to hospital each morning, I made sure that I ate a solid breakfast and took healthy food to eat during the day. Before the hospital concourse became filled with the bustle of the day, I would take time out to grab a comforting warm drink. During the day, I would go for brief walks outside the hospital, or take time out to ring my best friend in the world for a chat. These might all seem obvious or trivial examples, but they were all small and easily manageable actions, which all made crucial differences to my state of mind while I was undergoing a painful and worrying time. And they are the sorts of things people don't bother to do, to look after themselves when something traumatic is happening.

You NEED to keep watering YOU.

People will cross the road to avoid you when dark times fall. Mostly, this is only because they are worried about saying the wrong thing – try not to be hurt, even when a friend seems like they don't want to talk to you. However, there will always be people, like my friend Julie, who stay steadfast there on the garden path beside you and won't budge. Look out for those people, because they are invaluable to you and your wellbeing. And one day you will hopefully be able to repay their kindness, by being there when they are going through a difficult time.

After many years of dealing with some incredibly tough challenges, I could now be in a much worse place, both mentally and physically. The reason I'm not is because I kept watering myself. Even when I needed to give up work eventually to recover, a year after Rob died, it was because I knew I needed to 'water ME' some more.

I am now going to share with you a hugely valuable exercise, to help you discover your own good grief garden path. Following the few simple steps below will help you to survive the grieving process and to eventually reach the end of the path and flourish again in the sunshine.

Get some pens and paper to the ready, and get to work!

Exercise: YOUR wellbeing watering can

I would like you to imagine a watering can. This represents YOU.

I would like you to estimate, on a scale of 1 to 100, how full your watering can is, right now. By this, I mean in terms of how much energy you have, and how you are feeling. For example, as I write this, I reckon my can is approximately 80% full.

Part 1

Draw a watering can on a large piece of paper. Don't worry about your artistic skills! This is purely for you to be able to imagine a watering can and relate it to how you are feeling.

Next, colour the can in, to the level it is at this very moment, giving you a visual picture of how full it is now. You will know by looking at the can if your energy level – how well you are feeling – needs to be increased.

You are now ready to complete the next part of the exercise.

Part 2

When I talk about watering YOU, I am referring to the things that you need physically, mentally, emotionally and spiritually.

I now want you to start thinking about each these four things:

1. What do I need physically?
2. What do I need mentally?
3. What do I need emotionally?
4. What do I need spiritually?

Next, on the same or a new piece of paper, start jotting down the things that YOU need, to answer each of the questions above.

They can be very basic things. For example, in answer to the first question about what you need physically, you might write 'food and drink'. Next, I would like you to begin expanding on that. What kind of food and drink? What do you like or need to eat and drink? What makes you feel good, and (quite often a different answer) what does your body *need*, in terms of vitamins, fibre, protein, etc?

In response to this, I often get the joke 'Does wine water you?!' I have a complex answer to that, but the simple one is that drinking in moderation is great if you like it. However, we all know that drinking to excess can of course make you feel worse, both physically and mentally. The same applies of course to overeating. If you have in the past turned to excess eating or alcohol to blot out pain, it will help you to emphasise in your list the need to stick to healthy food and drink plans.

Answers to the other questions might include exercise, love, friends, relationships, people, fresh air, financial security, home, animals and being part of a community. But please don't just add those words – think of *everything* that you personally need, then expand on each area.

You can depict this list however you want – You might, for example, choose to make it into a picture or a map. A lot of people find it really helpful to be creative – how about using coloured pens, or creating a collage of images taken from magazines? The only important thing, though, is that you are happy with your final list. This isn't something you need to share with the world. It's all about YOU.

There's also no rush or time limit. After all these years in personal recovery – my own recovery and helping others – I still update and add to my wellbeing watering can exercise.

Good luck with yours. I hope you enjoy, finally, having a clear picture in front of you of what you need for your own wellbeing.

Part 3

Start to include everything you have listed in Part 2 into your **daily** life. The emphasis there is on 'daily'! You might find this hard at first, but I promise you the rewards will be worth it.

Even when you feel you can't bear to peek out from under your duvet or face the world ever again, I want you to keep this exercise in mind. **Do something from that list, every single day**.

'Keep watering YOU' isn't going to miraculously transport you away from your grief garden path. The path is a process you *need* to work through, in order to once more become healthy and happy. However, I promise this exercise will make the journey at least a little more bearable for you and even others around you. You will find it a little easier to get up in the morning and face the day ahead, and then one day the sun might shine, and you will notice the warmth of its rays.

A very important part of this exercise is to keep coming back to it. Every time you look at your watering can, you will be able to judge how full it is – how well you are feeling – at that new point in your life. You may well also identify new needs, things you can add to your wellbeing list, and be able to focus on new things that will make you feel healthier and happier.

Please keep watering YOU, for ever and a day. Your garden – your life – will always *need* tending and nurturing.

The good news

You have this coffee-table gift book to keep and refer to whenever you need it, and you can share it with everyone you know who needs to hear its messages. Helping other people will inevitably help you to feel better, too.

The garden path ahead

This is the end of this coffee-table gift book, and I genuinely hope it has been just that – a gift to YOU.

For some of you, the weather in your 'garden' – your life – may still be very stormy. For some it may be a bit dark and cloudy. For others, the rain may just be beginning to clear, and the sun may even just be starting to peek out from behind those clouds.

Please stop for a moment and think about what the weather is like for you.

If you are in the midst of a storm, I promise the rain will eventually begin to clear and there will be breaks in the clouds. The sun is always there, just not visible to some of you right now.

My hope for you is that one day you will be able to accept that your loved one will ALWAYS be with you. They have just gone to another part of your 'garden' – your life – where they will live for ever, in your heart and your mind.

Please take time to learn what you need in order to be healthy and happy, and keep focusing every single day on watering you. Doing this will ensure you somehow get through this journey and make yours a GOOD grief garden path.

I also hope that you will eventually be able to look back with a smile on your face rather than a tear in your eye, and with warmth in your heart replacing the pain you have felt.

Warmest wishes and love

Julie x

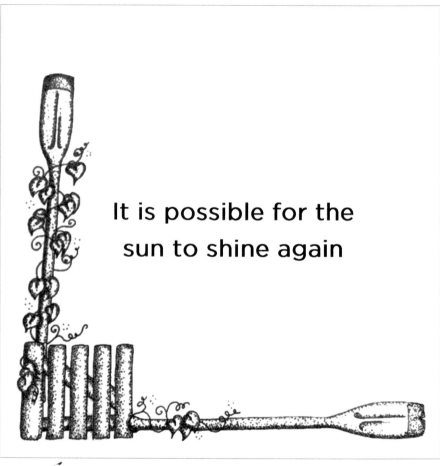

It is possible for the
sun to shine again

About the author

Julie New was a senior nurse and midwife until 2005, when she left the NHS and started training to become a personal recovery coach. She later became founder of and inspiration behind the organisation Changes Forever. It was and is her hope that Changes Forever will enable, inspire and support people to fully enjoy their lives and to become the best they possibly can.

Julie is kind, loving and fun to be with, and uses her own challenging life experiences to help other people to recover the happiness they deserve in their lives.

At the Changes Forever brand launch, a new member said: 'When I first heard Julie speak, I was puzzled; she doesn't come over like an evangelist, and yet I could simply see how much impact her message had on the people there and so many in the future.

'When I met her and sat down with her, I began to understand. She is passionate about personal growth, and her ideas about the garden. Her plans for Changes Forever bubble out, and you feel yourself wanting to help make that happen. She is completely sincere, and genuinely wants to reach as many people as possible, to help them to move through and beyond particularly difficult stages in their lives.

'But, above all, Julie exudes what psychologists call unconditional positive regard. She is genuinely interested in the people she meets; she values them, no matter who they are; and she is driven to make things better for them. You never know where you are going to land up, being with Julie, but you know it will be a great experience!'

Over the years, Julie has developed a unique, solutions-based personal recovery programme, designed to help anyone reconnect with themselves and with life, and to move forward in a positive way.

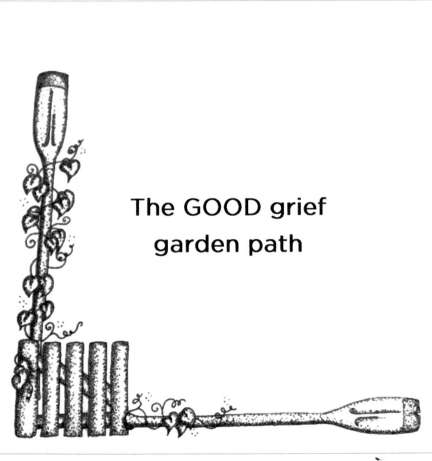

The GOOD grief
garden path

85

BV - #0038 - 290120 - C0 - 152/152/6 [8] - CB - 9781912243839